DISCOVERING Space

THE SUN

Ian Graham

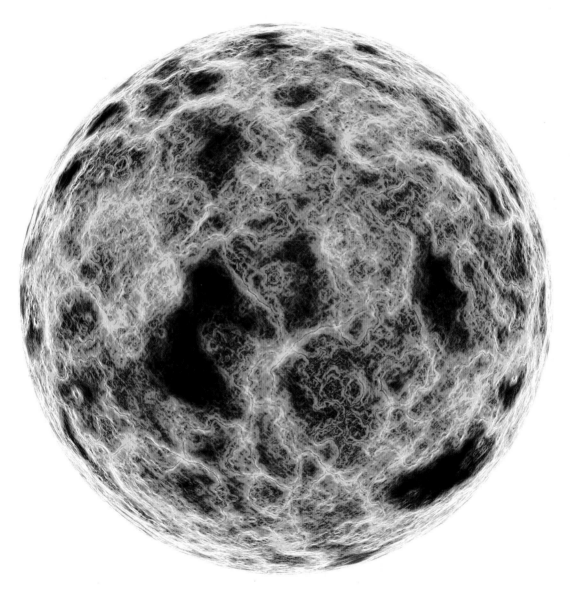

W
FRANKLIN WATTS

An Appleseed Editions book

First published in 2007 by Franklin Watts

Franklin Watts
338 Euston Road, London NW1 3BH

Franklin Watts Australia
Level 17/207 Kent St, Sydney, NSW 2000

Appleseed Editions Ltd
Well House, Friars Hill, Guestling, East Sussex TN35 4ET

Created by Q2A Creative
Series Editor: Honor Head
Designers: Diksha Khatri, Ashita Murgai
Picture Researchers: Lalit Dalal, Jyoti Sachdev

ISBN 978 0 7496 7545 5

Dewey classification: 523.7

All words in **bold** can be found in the glossary on page 30.

A CIP catalogue for this book is available from the British Library.

Picture credits
t=top b=bottom c=centre l=left r=right
Cover images: Courtesy of Science Photo Library / Photolibrary
NASA: 4b, Winfried Wisniewski/ zefa Corbis: 5 (background), NOAA /Grant W. Goodge: 5t, ESA: 6-7b, SOHO (ESA & NASA): 7t,
Bettmann/Corbis: 8b, JON LOMBERG/ Science Photo Library/ Photolibrary: 10t, NASA/MODIS/ USGS: 12b, Bryan F. Peterson/
Corbis: 13, SOHO (ESA & NASA): 14b, 14-15 (background), NASA: 15b, NASA, The Hubble Heritage Team,
STScI, AURA & HEIC: 16b. 16-17 (background), MARK GARLICK/ Science Photo Library/ Photolibrary: 17t, NASA/ JPL: 18c,
DavidHardy/ Science Photo Library/ Photolibrary: 19t, ESA: 20b, EIT Consortium (ESA/NASA): 21c, Copyright 1980 by Fred
Espenak,www.MrEclipse.com: 22t, NOAO/AURA/NSF: 22b, MARK GARLICK/ Science Photo Library/ Photolibrary: 22-23
(background),SOHO (ESA & NASA): 23t, Bill Livingston/NSO/AURA/NSF: 24b, Roger Ressmeyer/Corbis: 25, LYNETTE COOK/
Science Photo Library/ Photolibrary: 26b, A. Dupree (CfA), R. Gilliland (STScI), NASA: 27t.

Printed in China

Franklin Watts is a division of Hachette Children's Books

Contents

The Sun

Without the Sun, the Earth would be a dry, cold, brown, lifeless rock. The Sun provides us with light and heat which most living things need to survive. It warms the land and sea, so that moisture **evaporates** from the oceans, lakes and rivers to form rain clouds.

Our Solar System

The Sun is at the centre of a group of eight **planets**. The planets travel around the Sun. The paths they follow around the Sun are called orbits. The Sun, the planets, their **moons** and everything else orbiting the Sun are called the **Solar System**.

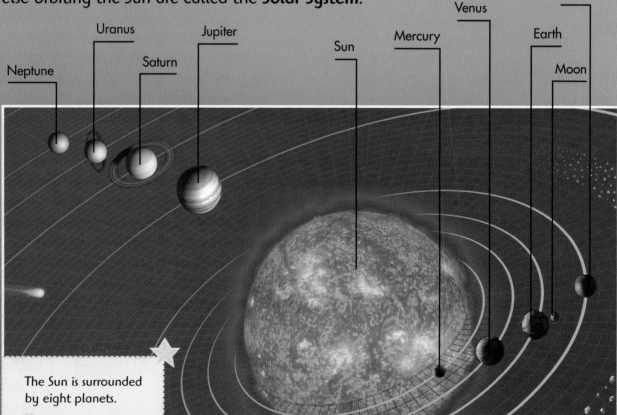

Neptune · Uranus · Saturn · Jupiter · Sun · Mercury · Venus · Mars · Earth · Moon

The Sun is surrounded by eight planets.

Pulling power

The Earth's **gravity** holds us down on the ground. The Sun has gravity, too, which holds the planets in their orbits. Without the Sun's gravity, the planets would go flying off into deep space and the Solar System would not exist.

The Sun sets in the west, lighting up the clouds in that direction.

Spotlight on
space

The Sun is the biggest object in the Solar System. It is more than a million times bigger than Earth. The Sun is so big that it contains 500 times more matter than everything else in the Solar System put together.

!

WARNING!
Never look straight at the Sun and never look at it through a camera, binoculars or a telescope. The light from the Sun is so strong it can make you go blind, even if you are wearing dark glasses.

Our star

The Sun is a **star** just like the many thousands of other stars in the sky. It looks bigger and brighter than all the other stars because it is closer to Earth. The Sun is our star. It is the only star in the Earth's Solar System.

Inside the Sun

The *SOHO* space probe has been finding out what happens inside the Sun by studying the waves that spread across the Sun, like ripples on a pond. These ripples give clues to what is happening inside the Sun.

SOHO mission

Launched	▶	2 December 1995
Orbit	▶	1.5 million kilometres away from the Earth facing the Sun
Size	▶	9.5 metres across its solar panels
Weight	▶	1,850 kilograms

Sun facts

Size across the middle	▶	1,392,000 kilometres
Mass	▶	as much as 333,000 Earths
Distance from Earth	▶	about 150 million kilometres

Spotlight on
space

It is hard to understand how far away the Sun is from Earth. The fastest way to travel on Earth is by jet plane. If you could fly a jet plane from the Earth to the Sun, it would take nearly 19 years to get there.

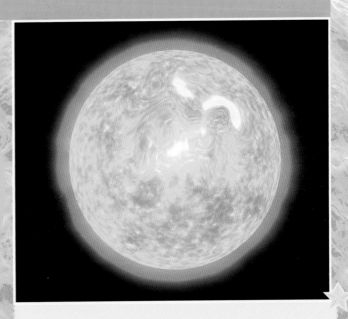

The *SOHO* space probe takes close-up pictures of the Sun and sends them to scientists on Earth.

The Sun is yellow because of its temperature. Hotter stars are blue or white. Cooler stars are red.

The giant Sun

The Sun looks like a small ball in the sky, but it is a giant compared to Earth. It is as wide as 109 Earths placed side by side. If you had a bag the size of the Sun, you would need more than a million Earths to fill it. And if you could put the Sun on one end of a seesaw, you would need 333,000 Earths on the other end to balance it.

The *SOHO* spacecraft uses 12 instruments to keep a constant watch on the Sun.

Myth and magic

People in ancient civilizations had some strange beliefs to explain the rising and setting of the Sun and its movement across the sky. They created stories to make sense of what they saw. One common idea was that the Sun rode across the sky in a chariot or boat.

Sky chariot

The Sun god of ancient Greece was called Helios. Every day Helios crossed the sky from east to west in a fiery chariot pulled by horses. Then he had to get back to the east for the next morning. So, during the night, he sailed through the ocean back to the east, out of sight inside a golden cup.

Sun gods

Many ancient civilizations had Sun gods.

		Name of Sun god
Egyptian	▶	Ra
Greek	▶	Helios
Roman	▶	Sol or Apollo
Hindu	▶	Surya
Inca	▶	Inti
Inuit	▶	Malina

Helios rode across the sky in a glowing chariot pulled by horses. The glowing Sun was Helios's fiery crown.

Ancient Egypt

More than 4,000 years ago, the ancient Egyptians worshipped a Sun god called Ra. They believed Ra sailed across the sky in a boat during the day. At night, he made his way back through the Underworld, ready to set sail across the sky again the next morning. They believed that in the Underworld Ra met Apopis, a demon. Every night Apopis fought with Ra, but he could not kill him, so Ra was able to appear in his boat every morning to start a new day.

In ancient Egypt, the Sun god Ra was shown with the Sun in his headdress.

Spotlight on
space

During winter, the Sun does not rise as high in the sky as it does in the summer. In some ancient civilizations people thought this might be because the Sun god had become ill and weak.

Telling time

People have used the Sun to measure time for thousands of years. The Sun rising and setting marks the beginning and end of each day. The position of the Sun in the sky during the day tells us the time of day. The Earth moving around the Sun creates the four seasons that make up a year.

As the Earth moves around the Sun, half of the Earth is in sunlight while the other half is in darkness.

Calendar facts

Every fourth year, one extra day is added to the end of February to make the calendar catch up with the Sun. The year with the extra day is called a leap year.

Length of a solar day	▶	24 hours
Length of a solar year	▶	365.24 days
Length of a calendar year	▶	365 days

Day and night

The Sun does not really move across the sky, it is the Earth that is always moving. The Earth is constantly spinning. When you are on the side of the Earth that faces the Sun, it is daytime. Then the Earth spins round until you are on the side that faces away from the Sun and this is when night-time begins.

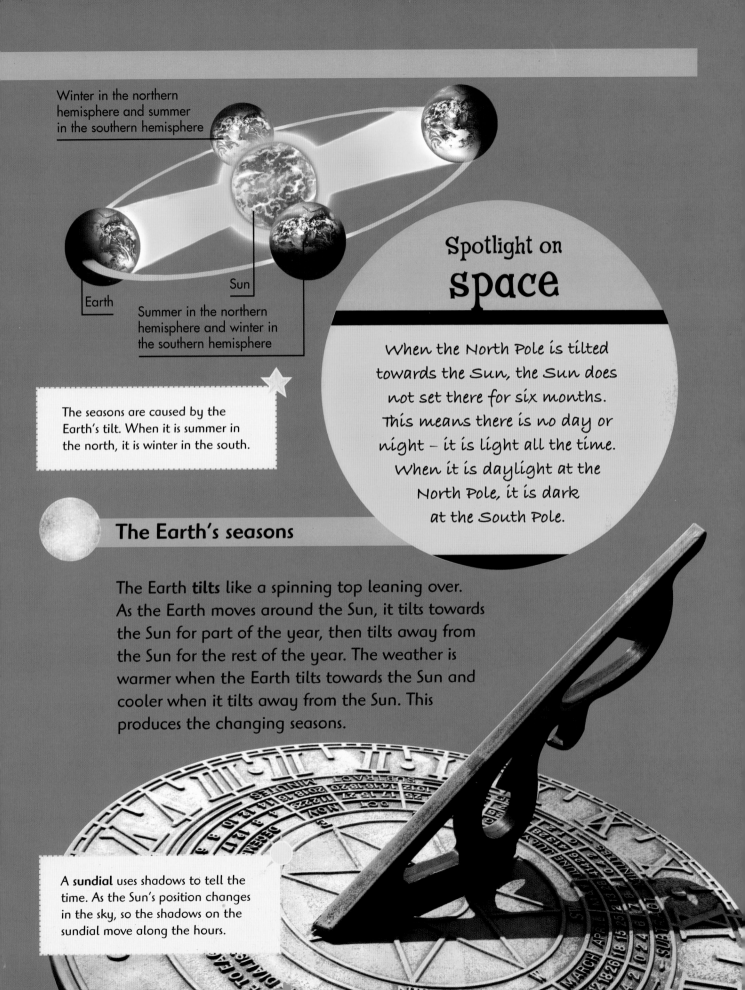

Winter in the northern hemisphere and summer in the southern hemisphere

Earth

Sun

Summer in the northern hemisphere and winter in the southern hemisphere

The seasons are caused by the Earth's tilt. When it is summer in the north, it is winter in the south.

Spotlight on space

When the North Pole is tilted towards the Sun, the Sun does not set there for six months. This means there is no day or night – it is light all the time. When it is daylight at the North Pole, it is dark at the South Pole.

The Earth's seasons

The Earth **tilts** like a spinning top leaning over. As the Earth moves around the Sun, it tilts towards the Sun for part of the year, then tilts away from the Sun for the rest of the year. The weather is warmer when the Earth tilts towards the Sun and cooler when it tilts away from the Sun. This produces the changing seasons.

A **sundial** uses shadows to tell the time. As the Sun's position changes in the sky, so the shadows on the sundial move along the hours.

Life giver

Four things are needed for life on Earth – light, warmth, oxygen and water. The Sun provides light and warmth which make green plants grow. Green plants make oxygen. The heat from the Sun causes evaporation which produces rain. This means Earth has a constant supply of water.

Life on Earth

If Earth was a lot closer to the Sun, all of its water would have boiled away long ago. If it was much further away from the Sun, its water would be solid ice. A planet needs to be the right distance from a star for life to be able to develop as it has on Earth. This distance is called the **life zone**.

Sunshine and water make life possible. Most of the Earth is covered by water.

Life zone

A planet needs to be a certain distance from a star for life to survive.

Closest	▶	120 million kilometres
Furthest	▶	240 million kilometres
Distance of Earth from the Sun	▶	150 million kilometres

Solar energy

Solar energy is the **energy** Earth receives from the Sun. Animals need this solar energy to live and grow, but they cannot use energy straight from the Sun. They get it by eating green plants or by eating other animals that live on green plants. Green plants take in energy from the Sun and use it for growth by a process called **photosynthesis**.

Earth receives just a tiny part of the huge amount of energy given out by the Sun but it is enough to support life on Earth.

Spotlight on
space

In only one hour, the Sun could supply the world with enough energy for everyone for a year. This would be the same amount of energy that we now get from coal, oil, gas and nuclear power stations.

Inside the Sun

The Sun is not solid like the Earth. There is no hard ground to walk on, even if you could survive the scorching heat. You cannot see through the Sun, but scientists have still managed to work out what it is like inside.

Heat and light

The heat and light that flow out from the Sun come from its **core**. Particles of **matter** at the centre of the Sun are so hot, and are squashed together so hard, that they stick to each other. This is called **nuclear fusion** and it gives out a lot of energy.

Heat and light escape into space

All the Sun's energy is produced at its core.

Energy travels outwards

Energy is produced in the Sun's core

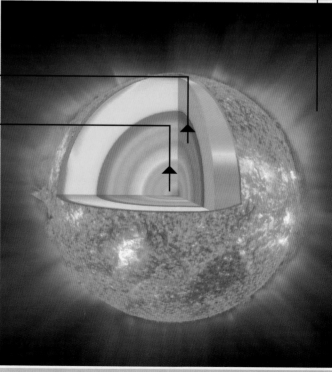

The Sun's heat

Temperature at core	▶	16 million degrees Celsius
Temperature at surface	▶	5,500 degrees Celsius

Spotlight on
space

The part of the Sun that we see is the part that gives out light. It is called the photosphere. It is also called the Sun's surface, although there is no solid ground. The photosphere is covered by hotter gas called the chromosphere. On top of this there is another layer of even hotter gas called the corona.

It takes hundreds of thousands of years for energy to go from the Sun's core to its surface, but it takes only eight minutes to reach Earth.

Boiling gas

Energy flows out in all directions from the Sun's core. Gas boils up to the surface, carrying the energy with it. When the energy escapes into space, the gas cools and sinks again. More hot gas rises to take its place. This makes the Sun's surface look like a pan of boiling water. Each of the bubbles of hot gas on the Sun is about 1,000 kilometres across.

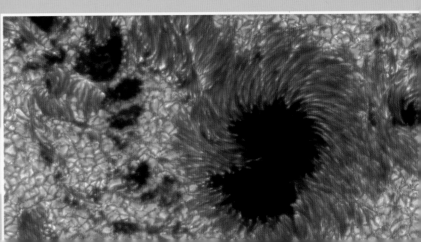

Gas boils up to the surface of the Sun around a dark **sunspot**.

The Sun's birth

There was a time, long ago, when there was no Sun. Instead, there was a giant cloud of gas and dust swirling in space. The Sun formed from this cloud about 4.5 billion years ago.

Spinning disc

The cloud began to collapse slowly, like a leaking party balloon. This happened because the cloud's own gravity pulled it inwards on itself. Then the whole cloud started spinning and became a flattened disc, like a spinning plate. Gas falling inwards made a big ball at the centre of the disc and this became the Sun.

A new Sun

Cloud collapsed for ▶	up to 1 million years
Sun heated up for ▶	50 million years
At last ▶	the cloud of heated gas became the Sun

A huge cloud of gas and dust like this gave birth to the Sun.

The Sun formed in the middle of a spinning disc of gas and dust.

Switching on

At first, the young Sun did not shine – it was just a big ball of gas. As more gas fell on to it, the Sun's gravity grew stronger. It squashed the gas at the centre harder and harder. The squashing heated the gas more and more and when it was hot enough the Sun became a dazzling star.

Spotlight on
space

The Sun shines because it changes matter into heat, light and other forms of energy. Every second the Sun loses about four million tonnes of matter. But it still has enough left to keep it shining for billions of years.

Scientists are trying to build power stations on Earth that work like the Sun. It may take another 50 years or more to get the first one working.

Wind in space

Particles of matter escape into space from the Sun all the time, like steam from boiling water. About a million tonnes of these particles fly out from the Sun every second. They go in all directions at great speed. This is called **solar wind**.

Capsule cover closes over base to protect it during return to Earth

Solar wind collectors

Re-entry capsule

The *Genesis* spacecraft has round dishes which trap solar wind particles.

Solar panel

Genesis

A spacecraft called *Genesis* was sent to collect solar wind particles and bring them back to Earth. The capsule with the particles inside crashed to the ground on Earth instead of landing safely but solar wind particles were still stored inside the dishes. Scientists are now studying them.

Genesis mission

Launched	▶	8 August 2001
Collection phase	▶	3 December 2001 to 2 April 2004
Returned to Earth	▶	8 September 2004

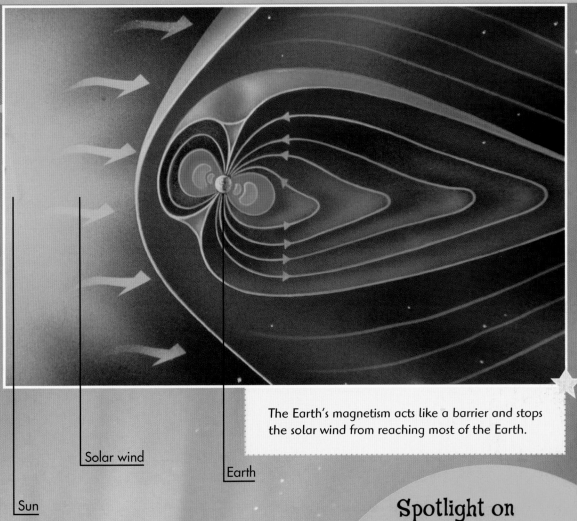

Sun

Solar wind

Earth

The Earth's magnetism acts like a barrier and stops the solar wind from reaching most of the Earth.

Sky lights

The solar wind travels all the way to Earth and far beyond. The Earth acts like a big magnet. Its magnetism pushes the solar wind away from the Earth except at the North and South Poles. When the solar wind hits the air above the Poles, it makes streaks of shimmering colours appear in the sky. This is called an **aurora**.

The solar wind travels amazingly fast. The slowest solar wind particles fly at 200 kilometres a second. The fastest travel at 1,000 kilometres a second. At this speed, you could zoom around the world in only 40 seconds.

An aurora lights up the sky as particles of the solar wind crash into air high above the ground.

Sun storms

From the Earth, the Sun looks like a plain yellow ball. But if you could get closer, you would see giant storms raging across the Sun. You would see its fiery surface boiling and giant streaks of gas flying out into space.

The Cluster mission

The *Cluster* mission sent four **satellites** into space to learn more about the solar wind and how Sun storms affect the Earth. It is the first time four spacecraft have ever flown through space together like this.

The four *Cluster* spacecraft study space weather.

Spotlight on
space

The first Cluster satellites were launched in 1996, but the rocket carrying them into space blew up and the satellites crashed to the ground. Four new satellites were launched four years later. This time they were launched two at a time by two rockets and the launches were successful.

Violent storms make the Sun's surface look like boiling fire.

Cluster mission

Launch of second *Cluster* mission ▷	16 July 2000 (2 satellites) 9 August 2000 (2 satellites)
Number of satellites ▷	4
Names of satellites ▷	*Rumba* *Salsa* *Samba* *Tango*
Orbit ▷	19,000–119,000 kilometres above Earth

Fountains of gas, bigger than the Earth, burst out of the Sun's surface.

Power cuts

Storms on the Sun sometimes fling huge amounts of gas out into space. This gas can fly in any direction. If the gas comes towards the Earth, it can cause power cuts and problems with radios and mobile phones. In 1989, a huge Sun storm caused power cuts in Canada. Scientists study the Sun every day, looking for signs of the next big storm that might affect us on Earth.

Studying the Sun

Scientists can study the Sun in two ways. They use telescopes on Earth and telescopes in space. Telescopes that study the Sun are called solar telescopes. They are specially designed for looking at the Sun without being damaged by its intense light and heat.

Solar scope

The McMath-Pierce telescope in the USA is a solar telescope. A mirror at the top of a tall tower reflects the Sun down a tunnel. The long tunnel goes underground. More mirrors in the tunnel reflect the Sun on to instruments which measure and record every detail.

McMath-Pierce solar telescope

Tower height ▶	30.5 metres
Length of tunnel ▶	152 metres
Size of Sun's image ▶	85 centimetres
Telescope opened ▶	1962

A mirror reflects light into the tunnel

The McMath-Pierce telescope is the world's biggest solar telescope.

Space telescopes

Some of the energy from the Sun cannot go through the Earth's **atmosphere**. If this energy does not reach the ground, telescopes on the ground cannot study it. So space scientists are now sending telescopes into space. The telescopes point at the Sun and send pictures and measurements back to Earth.

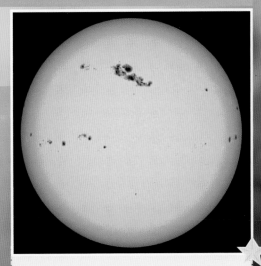

Dark spots, called sunspots, often appear on the Sun. Some last a few hours, others last for months.

Spotlight on
space

The Sun is magnetic. Sunspots are places where the Sun's magnetism becomes very strong for a while. Sunspots look dark because there is dazzling bright gas all around them. If you could look at a sunspot on its own, it would glow orange.

Sunspots have a dark centre called the umbra. The umbra has a lighter colour around it called the penumbra.

Eclipses

As the Earth and Moon move through space, they sometimes line up together with the Sun. These special events are called eclipses. When the Moon comes between the Earth and the Sun, it causes a **solar eclipse**.

Size and distance

The Sun is 400 times wider than the Moon and 400 times further away from the Earth than the Moon. This means that the Sun and Moon look roughly the same size from Earth, so when they line up, the Moon blots out the Sun.

Spotlight on space

When the Sun is almost covered by the Moon, beams of sunlight filter through the edges of the Moon. They make a line of bright spots called Baily's Beads, because they look like a string of beads. Sometimes there is just one dazzling spot and this is called a diamond ring, because that is what it looks like.

The 'diamond ring' sparkles during a total eclipse.

Biting the Sun

Total eclipses cannot be seen from everywhere on Earth. You can only see a total eclipse from certain places. These places are where the darkest part of the Moon's shadow falls during an eclipse. Outside the darkest part of the shadow, the Moon covers only part of the Sun and the Sun looks as if someone has taken a bite out of it. This is called a partial eclipse.

When the Moon covers the Sun, the glowing gas around the Sun suddenly becomes visible.

Future solar eclipses

Date of eclipse	Will be seen from
1 August 2008	Arctic Ocean, Siberia, China
22 July 2009	India, China, South Pacific Ocean
11 July 2010	South Pacific Ocean
13 November 2012	Northern Australia, South Pacific Ocean

The future

The Sun will not last forever. Two forces are balanced in the Sun – gravity and heat. Gravity pulls inwards and tries to make the Sun smaller. The Sun's heat pushes back and tries to make it bigger. If the Sun ever cools down, gravity will make the Sun collapse in on itself.

The dying Sun

The Sun produces heat and light by slamming small particles of matter together to make bigger, heavier particles of matter. After a very long time, the particles of matter become so big that the Sun cannot slam them together hard enough any more. When this happens, the core of the Sun will stop producing heat and the Sun will start to die.

The Sun's life cycle

Formed	▶	4.5 billion years ago
Shines for	▶	nearly 10 billion years
Will die	▶	about 5 billion years from now

In the far distant future, the dying Sun might look like this.

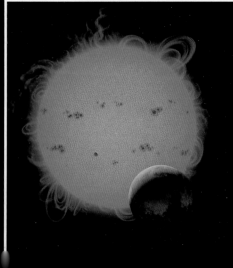

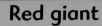
When the Sun stops making heat, its core will cool down and gravity will pull the Sun inwards on itself. As the core gets smaller, the outer layers of the Sun will swell up and cool. The cooling gas will change from bright yellow to red as the Sun dies. The huge dying Sun will become a **red giant**. Finally, the gas around the outside of the Sun will drift away into space. A tiny star called a **white dwarf** will be left behind.

Betelgeuse is a red giant more than 500 times wider than the Sun. It is so big that it is called a supergiant.

Spotlight on
space

What will happen to the Earth when the Sun dies? As it dies, the Earth will get hotter and hotter. Life on Earth will become impossible. Eventually, the Earth will fall into the Sun and burn up. Scientists say that this is likely to happen in about five billion years.

The Sun will shine for billions of years before it starts to fade away.

Timeline

4.5 billion years ago
The Sun is formed from a cloud of gas and dust.

1223 BC
A solar eclipse is recorded on a piece of clay.

800 BC
A Chinese book, called the *Book of Changes*, includes a description of a sunspot.

270 BC
The Greek astronomer Aristarchus of Samos says the Sun is at the centre of the Solar System, but no one believes him.

AD 140
The Egyptian astronomer Ptolemy says that the Earth is at the centre of the Solar System and everyone believes him.

1543
The Polish astronomer Nicolaus Copernicus writes a book which describes the Solar System with the Sun at its centre.

1610
Thomas Harriot, an English mathematician, is the first person to study sunspots with a telescope.

1611
The Italian astronomer Galileo Galilei sees sunspots on the Sun.

1633
Galileo says that Copernicus was right and the Sun is at the centre of the Solar System. Galileo is later forced to reject the idea by the Roman Catholic Church.

1668
English astronomer Isaac Newton makes the first reflecting telescope.

1727
Swedish astronomer Anders Celsius and Englishman George Graham see a magnetic storm on the Sun.

1754
Englishman John Dollond invents an instrument called a heliometer and uses it to measure the width of the Sun.

1769
In Tahiti, an island in the Pacific Ocean, English explorer Captain Cook sees the planet Venus crossing in front of the Sun.

1800
English astronomer William Herschel discovers that the Sun gives out invisible infra-red (heat) rays.

1801
English scientist William Wollaston spreads out sunlight into all of its colours and sees dark lines in the colours.

1815
German scientist Joseph von Fraunhofer does the same experiment as Wollaston. He finds the same dark lines in the rainbow of colours in sunlight. Later, these dark lines help scientists to find out what the Sun is made of.

1845
The first photographs of the Sun are taken.

1851
The first photograph of a total solar eclipse is taken.

1870
The first photograph of a Sun storm, called a prominence, is taken.

1938
Scientists work out why the Sun shines.

1942
Scientists discover that the Sun gives out radio waves.

1958
American scientist Eugene Parker thinks there is a solar wind of particles blowing through space from the Sun. Few scientists agree with him. They think space is empty.

1959
The Russian space probe *Luna I* discovers the solar wind.

1962
The McMath-Pierce solar telescope begins observations of the Sun.

1973
Astronauts on board the US space station *Skylab* begin studying the Sun and filming it from space.

1980
The *Solar Maximum Mission* satellite is launched to study the Sun when it is especially stormy.

1989
Storms on the Sun cause power cuts lasting five hours in Canada.

1990
The *Ulysses* space probe is launched to study the Sun by flying over its poles.

1992
After more than 350 years, the Roman Catholic church accepts that Galileo was right when he said that the Sun is at the centre of the Solar System.

1995
The *SOHO* solar space probe is launched.

1996
The four satellites of the *Cluster* mission are destroyed when their *Ariane 5* rocket explodes.

1998
The *TRACE* space probe is launched to observe the Sun.

2000
Four new *Cluster* mission satellites are launched by two Russian rockets.

2001
The US *Genesis* space probe is launched to collect particles of the solar wind and bring them back to Earth.

2004
The *Genesis* space probe brings particles of the solar wind back to Earth, but crashes into the ground.

5 billion years from now
The Sun will swell up into a red giant and then shrink to become a white dwarf star.

Glossary

atmosphere The gases that surround most planets, some moons and stars.

aurora Streaks of different coloured lights seen in the sky, especially at the North Pole and South Pole.

calendar year A time period of 12 calendar months lasting 365 days, or 366 days in a leap year.

core The centre of a planet or star.

energy We need energy to live. There are many forms of energy, including heat and light.

evaporates Turns from water into vapour when heated by the Sun. The water rises into the air where it forms rain clouds.

gravity An invisible force that pulls things towards each other. Earth's gravity pulls us down to the ground. The Sun's gravity keeps the Earth and other planets going around the Sun.

Inuit Another name for Eskimos, especially those from Greenland and Canada.

life zone The distance a planet must be from a star for life to have a chance of developing.

mass Something that all matter has. The more mass something has, the heavier it is.

matter The particles that gases, liquids and solid objects are made of.

moons Small objects orbiting a planet. The Earth has one moon.

nuclear fusion The process inside the Sun that produces energy by smashing small particles of matter together to make bigger particles.

photosynthesis The process used by plants to turn sunlight into food.

planets Large round objects in orbit around a star.

power stations Large buildings used to produce electricity.

red giant A star that has swollen up and turned red near the end of its life.

satellites Moons in orbit around a planet, or spacecraft in orbit around a planet or moon.

SOHO Solar and Heliospheric Observatory.

solar eclipse An event that happens when the Moon passes between the Sun and Earth.

solar energy Heat, light and other energy given out by the Sun.

Solar System The Sun, planets, moons and everything else that orbits the Sun.

solar wind Particles that fly out of the Sun into space in all directions.

solar year The time the Earth takes to go round the Sun once.

space probe An unmanned spacecraft sent from Earth to explore space.

star Huge glowing ball of gas. The Sun is a star.

sundial An instrument for telling the time by a shadow cast by the Sun.

sunspot A dark mark that appears on the Sun.

tilts Leans to one side slightly.

white dwarf A tiny star only about as big as the Earth, formed when a star like the Sun comes to the end of its life.

Index

WEBFINDER

http://www.bbc.co.uk/science/space/solarsystem/sun/index.shtml

http://www.nasa.gov/vision/universe/solarsystem/sun_for_kids_main.html

http://observe.arc.nasa.gov/nasa/exhibits/sun/sunframe.html

http://starchild.gsfc.nasa.gov/docs/StarChild/solar_system_level1/sun.html

http://www.nationalgeographic.com/solarsystem/ax/low.html?2d

www.kidsastronomy.com/our_sun.htm

http://www.astronomytoday.com/astronomy/sun.html

http://www.noao.edu/image_gallery/solar.html